Grandad's Surprise

Written by Abi Wainwright
Illustrated by Jenny Palmer

Annika and Sanjay are the Hunter Kids!

Little Krishnan likes to help.

The Hunter Kids were visiting Granny and Grandad. They had a house far from the city.

"I am planning a surprise for you," Grandad said. "Will you help me find the last few things I need?"

"We are great at finding things!" said Annika excitedly.

"First we need long, strong things," said Grandad, pushing a wheelbarrow down to the woods.

"Trees are strong," said Sanjay.
"They are too big to carry!" Annika laughed.

Just then, Krishnan handed Annika a twig.

"Stick!" he said proudly.

"That gives me a thought," said Annika. "Could we use these fallen branches?"

"Great!" said Grandad.

"Is it a surprise bonfire?" asked Sanjay.
"No," said Grandad.

They went along the canal until they got to the boatyard.

"The next thing we need must be see-through," said Grandad.

Sanjay saw an object sparkling in the sun.

"A porthole window!" he said.
"We can look through the glass."
"Very nice!" said Grandad.

"Is it for a telescope?" asked Annika.

"No, that's not it," said Grandad. "Now I just need a long, strong piece of rope …"

Annika saw some rope sticking out of a bucket.

She lifted it out and asked, "Will this do?"

"Perfect!" said Grandad.

Back at home, Grandad spent all afternoon working on his surprise.

The kids were painting with Granny but they could not stop thinking about it!

Just then, Grandad called them to join him in the garden.

Sanjay spotted the porthole glinting in the branches.

Annika saw the rope swaying in the distance.

What could it be?

"A treehouse!" shouted Sanjay, running over to it.

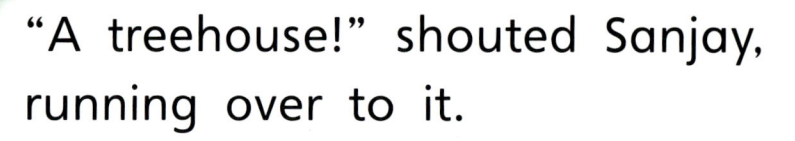

It had a roof with bunting, a spy window and a swing!

15

It was the perfect Hunter Kids den!